C000257344

2016 SQA Past Papers With Answers

Higher
GRAPHIC COMMUNICATION

2014 Specimen Question Paper, 2015 & 2016 Exams

SQA

Higher GRAPHIC COMMUNICATION

HODDER GIBSON
AN HACHETTE UK COMPANY

This book contains the official 2014 SQA Specimen Question Paper, 2015 and 2016 Exams for Higher Graphic Communication, with associated SQA-approved answers modified from the official marking instructions that accompany the paper.

In addition the book contains study skills advice. This advice has been specially commissioned by Hodder Gibson, and has been written by experienced senior teachers and examiners in line with the new Higher for CfE syllabus and assessment outlines. This is not SQA material but has been devised to provide further guidance for Higher examinations.

Hodder Gibson is grateful to the copyright holders, as credited on the final page of the Answer Section, for permission to use their material. Every effort has been made to trace the copyright holders and to obtain their permission for the use of copyright material. Hodder Gibson will be happy to receive information allowing us to rectify any error or omission in future editions.

Hachette UK's policy is to use papers that are natural, renewable and recyclable products and made from wood grown in sustainable forests. The logging and manufacturing processes are expected to conform to the environmental regulations of the country of origin.

Orders: please contact Bookpoint Ltd, 130 Park Drive, Milton Park, Abingdon, Oxon OX14 4SE. Telephone: (44) 01235 827720. Fax: (44) 01235 400454. Lines are open 9.00–5.00, Monday to Saturday, with a 24-hour message answering service. Visit our website at www.hoddereducation.co.uk. Hodder Gibson can be contacted direct on: Tel: 0141 333 4650; Fax: 0141 404 8188; email: hoddergibson@hodder.co.uk

This collection first published in 2016 by
Hodder Gibson, an imprint of Hodder Education,
An Hachette UK Company
211 St Vincent Street
Glasgow G2 5QY

Higher 2014 Specimen Question Paper and Answers; Higher 2015 and 2016 Exam Papers and Answers © Scottish Qualifications Authority. Model Question Papers, Answers and Study Skills section © Hodder Gibson. All rights reserved. Apart from any use permitted under UK copyright law, no part of this publication may be reproduced or transmitted in any form or by any means, electronic or mechanical, including photocopying and recording, or held within any information storage and retrieval system, without permission in writing from the publisher or under licence from the Copyright Licensing Agency Limited. Further details of such licences (for reprographic reproduction) may be obtained from the Copyright Licensing Agency Limited, Saffron House, 6–10 Kirby Street, London EC1N 8TS.

Typeset by Aptara, Inc.

Printed in the UK

A catalogue record for this title is available from the British Library

ISBN: 978-1-4718-9091-8

3 2 1

2017 2016

Introduction

Study Skills – what you need to know to pass exams!

Pause for thought

Many students might skip quickly through a page like this. After all, we all know how to revise. Do you really though?

Think about this:

"IF YOU ALWAYS DO WHAT YOU ALWAYS DO, YOU WILL ALWAYS GET WHAT YOU HAVE ALWAYS GOT."

Do you like the grades you get? Do you want to do better? If you get full marks in your assessment, then that's great! Change nothing! This section is just to help you get that little bit better than you already are.

There are two main parts to the advice on offer here. The first part highlights fairly obvious things which are also very important. The second part makes suggestions about revision that you might not have thought about but which WILL help you.

Part 1

DOH! It's so obvious but …

Start revising in good time

Don't leave it until the last minute – this will make you panic.

Make a revision timetable that sets out work time AND play time.

Sleep and eat!

Obvious really, and very helpful. Avoid arguments or stressful things too – even games that wind you up. You need to be fit, awake and focused!

Know your place!

Make sure you know exactly WHEN and WHERE your exams are.

Know your enemy!

Make sure you know what to expect in the exam.

How is the paper structured?

How much time is there for each question?

What types of question are involved?

Which topics seem to come up time and time again?

Which topics are your strongest and which are your weakest?

Are all topics compulsory or are there choices?

Learn by DOING!

There is no substitute for past papers and practice papers – they are simply essential! Tackling this collection of papers and answers is exactly the right thing to be doing as your exams approach.

Part 2

People learn in different ways. Some like low light, some bright. Some like early morning, some like evening / night. Some prefer warm, some prefer cold. But everyone uses their BRAIN and the brain works when it is active. Passive learning – sitting gazing at notes – is the most INEFFICIENT way to learn anything. Below you will find tips and ideas for making your revision more effective and maybe even more enjoyable. What follows gets your brain active, and active learning works!

Activity 1 – Stop and review

Step 1

When you have done no more than 5 minutes of revision reading STOP!

Step 2

Write a heading in your own words which sums up the topic you have been revising.

Step 3

Write a summary of what you have revised in no more than two sentences. Don't fool yourself by saying, 'I know it but I cannot put it into words'. That just means you don't know it well enough. If you cannot write your summary, revise that section again, knowing that you must write a summary at the end of it. Many of you will have notebooks full of blue/black ink writing. Many of the pages will not be especially attractive or memorable so try to liven them up a bit with colour as you are reviewing and rewriting. **This is a great memory aid, and memory is the most important thing.**

Activity 2 – Use technology!

Why should everything be written down? Have you thought about 'mental' maps, diagrams, cartoons and colour to help you learn? And rather than write down notes, why not record your revision material?

What about having a text message revision session with friends? Keep in touch with them to find out how and what they are revising and share ideas and questions.

Why not make a video diary where you tell the camera what you are doing, what you think you have learned and what you still have to do? No one has to see or hear it but the process of having to organise your thoughts in a formal way to explain something is a very important learning practice.

Be sure to make use of electronic files. You could begin to summarise your class notes. Your typing might be slow but it will get faster and the typed notes will be easier to read than the scribbles in your class notes. Try to add different fonts and colours to make your work stand out. You can easily Google relevant pictures, cartoons and diagrams which you can copy and paste to make your work more attractive and MEMORABLE.

Activity 3 – This is it. Do this and you will know lots!

Step 1

In this task you must be very honest with yourself! Find the SQA syllabus for your subject (www.sqa.org.uk). Look at how it is broken down into main topics called MANDATORY knowledge. That means stuff you MUST know.

Step 2

BEFORE you do ANY revision on this topic, write a list of everything that you already know about the subject. It might be quite a long list but you only need to write it once. It shows you all the information that is already in your long-term memory so you know what parts you do not need to revise!

Step 3

Pick a chapter or section from your book or revision notes. Choose a fairly large section or a whole chapter to get the most out of this activity.

With a buddy, use Skype, Facetime, Twitter or any other communication you have, to play the game "If this is the answer, what is the question?". For example, if you are revising Geography and the answer you provide is "meander", your buddy would have to make up a question like "What is the word that describes a feature of a river where it flows slowly and bends often from side to side?".

Make up 10 "answers" based on the content of the chapter or section you are using. Give this to your buddy to solve while you solve theirs.

Step 4

Construct a wordsearch of at least 10 × 10 squares. You can make it as big as you like but keep it realistic. Work together with a group of friends. Many apps allow you to make wordsearch puzzles online. The words and phrases can go in any direction and phrases can be split. Your puzzle must only contain facts linked to the topic you are revising. Your task is to find 10 bits of information to hide in your puzzle but you must not repeat information that you used in Step 3. DO NOT show where the words are. Fill up empty squares with random letters. Remember to keep a note of where your answers are hidden but do not show your friends. When you have a complete puzzle, exchange it with a friend to solve each other's puzzle.

Step 5

Now make up 10 questions (not "answers" this time) based on the same chapter used in the previous two tasks. Again, you must find NEW information that you have not yet used. Now it's getting hard to find that new information! Again, give your questions to a friend to answer.

Step 6

As you have been doing the puzzles, your brain has been actively searching for new information. Now write a NEW LIST that contains only the new information you have discovered when doing the puzzles. Your new list is the one to look at repeatedly for short bursts over the next few days. Try to remember more and more of it without looking at it. After a few days, you should be able to add words from your second list to your first list as you increase the information in your long-term memory.

FINALLY! Be inspired...

Make a list of different revision ideas and beside each one write THINGS I HAVE tried, THINGS I WILL try and THINGS I MIGHT try. Don't be scared of trying something new.

And remember – FAIL TO PREPARE AND PREPARE TO FAIL!

Higher Graphic Communication

The course

The aims of the course are to enable you to understand how graphic communication is used every day in industry and society and to develop skills and techniques used in creating graphics to suit a range of functions and purposes.

The types of graphics you will learn about include:

- **Preliminary** design graphics
- Technical **production** drawings
- High impact **promotional** graphics.

These are known as the **3Ps**. Your coursework projects and exam questions are based on these types of graphics and the impact graphics have on society and the environment. The knowledge you need for the exam will come from the work you do during your project work in class.

How you are assessed and graded

The grade you achieve at the end of your course depends on a number of assessments.

Unit Assessment

Both Units (2D Graphics and 3D and Pictorial Graphics) are assessed on a pass or fail basis.

Both Units must be passed in order to qualify for a course award.

Course Assessment

The grade for the Higher course is derived from two course assessments:

- **The assignment**

This is the project you will complete towards the second half of your course and it is worth **70 marks**.

- **The exam paper**

The course exam paper is also worth **70 marks**.

The total, 140 marks, is graded from A to D for a pass.

The exam

The exam is **two hours** long and is worth a total of **70 marks**. It will include a mix of short questions and more extended questions relating to preliminary, production and promotional graphics. There will be different types of graphics to interpret and understand before questions can be answered. These graphics can be complex and detailed and it would be a mistake to jump straight in with answers. It is vital to spend time studying the graphics and the questions first.

Look at the marks awarded for each question. This is a good indicator of the length of answer you should give.

For example, a 3-mark question will need you to make three distinct points, while a 1-mark question may require only a single point. Each mark should take around 1 ½ minutes to earn with some reading time left over, so plan your time accordingly.

Sketching

Exam questions will be set so that you can answer in writing. However, some questions will invite you to answer using annotated sketches or drawings and space will be left so that you may sketch your answer. **Always take this opportunity.**

Remember:

- This is an exam about graphics and you have all the graphic skills you need.
- It is easier and quicker to describe your answer graphically with annotations.
- The quality of sketching will not be assessed but the clarity of your answer is important so make the sketches and annotations clear.
- Plan your sketches in a light pencil and firm in with a black pen.

Answering 3D CAD modelling questions

You should always:

- study the model and any other sketches, drawings or notes.
- identify what modelling techniques have been used (extrude, revolve, loft, helices or extrude along a path).
- describe the steps such as: new sketch, draw profile, select axis and revolve, etc.
- include reference to the dimensions provided.
- describe any additional edits used: array, subtract, shell, etc.
- and importantly, make sketches to help describe the steps.
- ensure your sketches are firmed in and outlined in pen to enable scanning of your answers.

Answering creative layout questions

These questions will ask you to identify how DTP features and design elements and principles have been used in a layout. You will always be asked to explain how the use of these features improves the layout. You should always:

- study the layout: don't rush this.
- identify the DTP features or elements and principles used.

- think carefully about how it improves the layout: does it add contrast, create harmony, suggest depth, develop a dominant focal point, unify the layout, create emphasis or connect or separate parts? The feature you are asked about will do one or more of these things. Your task is to spot which and explain how.

At the end of the exam, read over your answers and read the questions again. Double-check that you have answered the question. You should have plenty of time.

Skills and knowledge

The skills and knowledge the exam will test are:

Problem solving: explain how you would model, render or assemble a 3D CAD model or create a 2D CAD drawing.

Creative skills: describe how the graphic designer used design elements and principles to create an effective layout.

DTP features and edits: explain how the graphic designer used DTP features to achieve an effective layout.

Advantages and disadvantages: justify the best methods to choose when creating graphics.

Knowledge of drawing standards: explain how drawing standards should be applied to orthographic and pictorial drawings including technical detail.

Spatial awareness: testing your ability to interpret and understand drawings.

Graphics in society: explain how graphics are used in society.

Graphics and the environment: explain how we can create and use graphics without damaging our fragile environment.

Practising the type of questions you are likely to face in the Higher exam is vital. This book will give you experience of the problem solving and creative layout questions you will experience in the exam. Ensure you tackle these important sections before your prelim and course exams.

Good luck!

Remember that the rewards for passing Higher Graphic Communication are well worth it! Your pass will help you get the future you want for yourself. In the exam, be confident in your own ability. If you're not sure how to answer a question, trust your instincts and just give it a go anyway. Keep calm and don't panic! GOOD LUCK!

HIGHER

2014 Specimen Question Paper

H

National
Qualifications
SPECIMEN ONLY

SQ22/H/01

Graphic Communication

Date — Not applicable

Duration — 2 hours

Fill in these boxes and read what is printed below.

Full name of centre

Town

Forename(s)

Surname

Number of seat

Date of birth
Day   Month   Year

D D   M M   Y Y

Scottish candidate number

Total marks — 70

Attempt ALL questions.

Write your answers clearly in the spaces provided in this booklet. Additional space for answers is provided at the end of this booklet. If you use this space you must clearly identify the question number you are attempting.

All dimensions are in mm.

All technical sketches and drawings use third angle projection.

You may use rulers, compasses or trammels for measuring.

In all questions you may use sketches and annotations to support your answer if you wish.

Use **blue** or **black** ink.

Before leaving the examination room you must give this booklet to the Invigilator; if you do not, you may lose all the marks for this paper.

Attempt ALL questions

Total marks — 70

MARKS | DO NOT WRITE IN THIS MARGIN

1. A public building that was constructed in the 1950s is to be modernised. The original drawings were produced manually in paper format. The architect has requested that the manual drawings be converted to a digital format and sent electronically.

   The conversion methods being considered are: scanning the original drawings **or** reproducing the drawings using CAD software.

   (a) (i) Compare the two methods in terms of their suitability for this task.

   4

1. (a) (continued)

    (ii) Explain two possible disadvantages that may be encountered when two different people or companies work together on the same project using CAD.

2

CAD simulation could be used to test aspects of the design of the building.

(b) Identify an aspect of the design that could be tested through a CAD simulation.

1

(c) Identify an advantage of a "paperless office" to an architectural business.

1

MARKS | DO NOT WRITE IN THIS MARGIN

2. The sketches below were used by a CAD technician to create a 3D model of a portable speaker casing. The 3D model will be used to make production drawings and a promotional illustration.

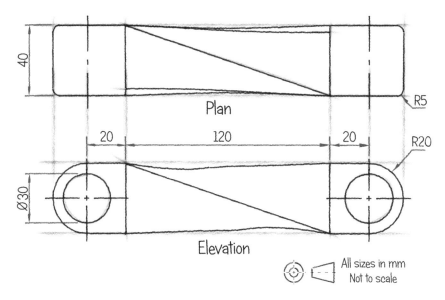

Orthographic sketch

The CAD technician sketched a modelling plan before creating the 3D model. The first two stages of the modelling plan are shown below.

(a) Describe the 3D modelling techniques proposed for each stage, making reference to all relevant dimensions from the orthographic sketch. You can sketch, annotate the sketches provided and/or use text in your answer.

(i)

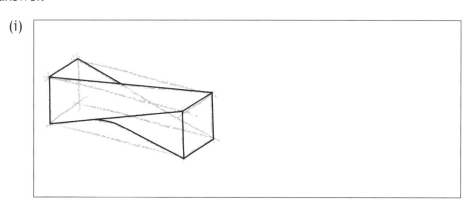

2

(ii)

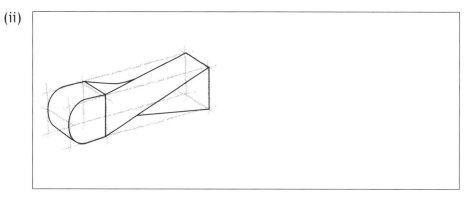

2

MARKS

2. **(continued)**

Solid model of the
portable speaker casing

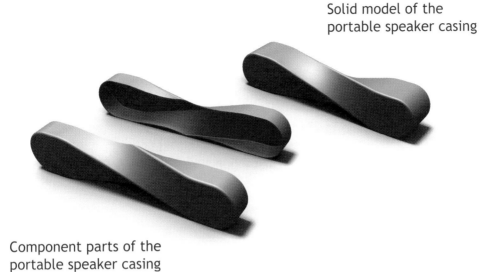

Component parts of the
portable speaker casing

A solid model of the portable speaker casing and the two components generated from it are shown above.

(b) Describe, using a "top-down" approach, the techniques used to create the two component parts from the solid model. You can sketch, annotate and/or use text in your answer.

4

MARKS | DO NOT WRITE IN THIS MARGIN

2.   (continued)

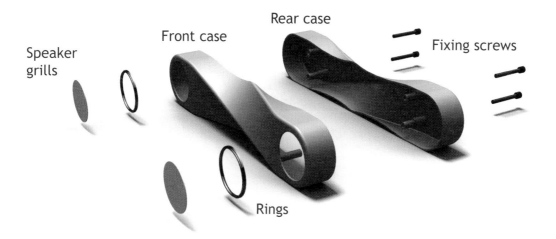

Speaker grills

Front case

Rear case

Fixing screws

Rings

The components of the speaker casing are shown above.

The fixing screws were imported from a CAD library.

(c)   Explain why this type of component would be included in a CAD library.   **2**

2.   (continued)

The two component parts of the portable speaker casing need to be assembled within the CAD software.

(d) Outline the 3D modelling techniques used to fully constrain the two component parts. You may use annotated sketches to support your answer if you wish.

2

2.   (continued)

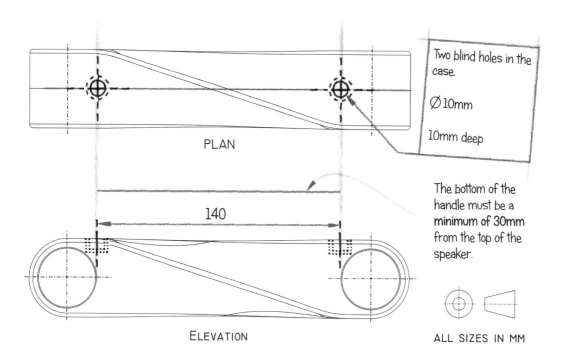

PLAN

140

ELEVATION

Two blind holes in the case.

Ø10mm

10mm deep

The bottom of the handle must be a minimum of 30mm from the top of the speaker.

ALL SIZES IN MM

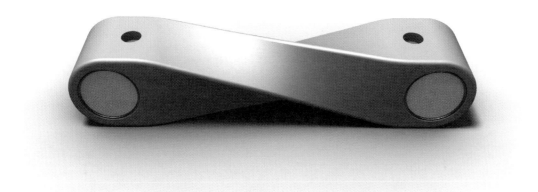

MARKS | DO NOT WRITE IN THIS MARGIN

2. **(continued)**

The portable speaker casing design has been modified to allow a simple handle to be attached. These modifications have been sketched on the production drawings and shown on the 3D model on the left.

(e) Produce a modelling plan which could be used to create a 3D CAD model of a simple handle to fit the blind holes in the casing. The handle will be glued into the holes. You can sketch, annotate, and/or use text in your answer.

4

MARKS | DO NOT WRITE IN THIS MARGIN

3. The promotional layout below is used to attract consumers to a new product.

The BIO+ball is an innovative new product that helps to ensure the well being of you and your family.

Whilst the BIO+ball is innocently floating around in the kitchen sink it is constantly killing off harmful germs.

BIO+ball is so versatile that is can be used when cleaning dishes, preparing vegetables and when washing hands.

Explain how the graphic designer has used typeface, colour and choice of images to attract consumers.

4

4. Components that make up a pulley wheel assembly are shown below as an exploded view.

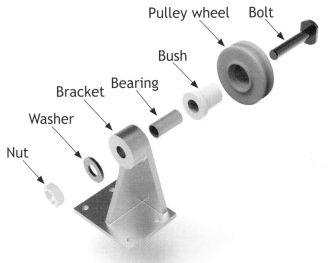

An incomplete sectional elevation, cut along a central vertical plane, is shown below.

(a) (i) Apply hatching to the assembled elevation to show the different components taking account of British Standards. You may sketch the section lines on the view and you can use a straight edge if you wish.   3

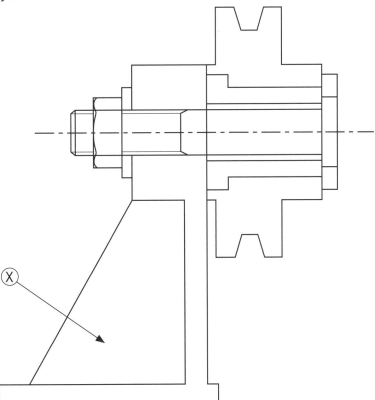

   (ii) State the name for the feature shown at X.   1

_____

4. (a) (continued)

The bolt used in the assembly has flat sections on the end for a spanner to fit.

(iii) Apply the British Standards convention for this flat on the bolt shown below (Figure 1).

1

Figure 1   **Figure 2**

The 3D view in Figure 2 shows the pulley assembly bolted by the base to another component. The drawing below shows the three stages.

Stage 1 — a blind hole is machined in the component

Stage 2 — a thread is cut into the blind hole

Stage 3 — an M10 bolt and washer is fitted to secure the pulley assembly

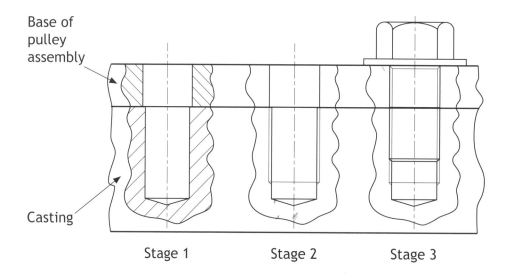

Stage 1   Stage 2   Stage 3

(b) (i) Apply hatching to **Stage 2** and **Stage 3** above taking account of British Standards and conventions. You may sketch the section lines on the view and you can use a straight edge if you wish.

2

MARKS | DO NOT WRITE IN THIS MARGIN

4. (b) (continued)

(ii) Explain the term "blind hole" at Stage 1.

1

(iii) What does the "M" stand for on the M10 bolt?

1

(iv) Determine the depth of the hole for the thread cut at Stage 2.

1

(v) State the type of section shown at Stages 1 to 3.

1

The holes on the base of the pulley assembly are 10·5 mm with a tolerance of −0·15 and +0·15 applied.

(vi) Apply the dimensional tolerance to the hole in Stage 1 taking account of British Standards.

1

5. The elevation of two interpenetrating cylindrical pipes is shown below. A surface development of interpenetrating cylindrical pipes is being generated using 2D CAD. The elevation and part construction work is shown below.

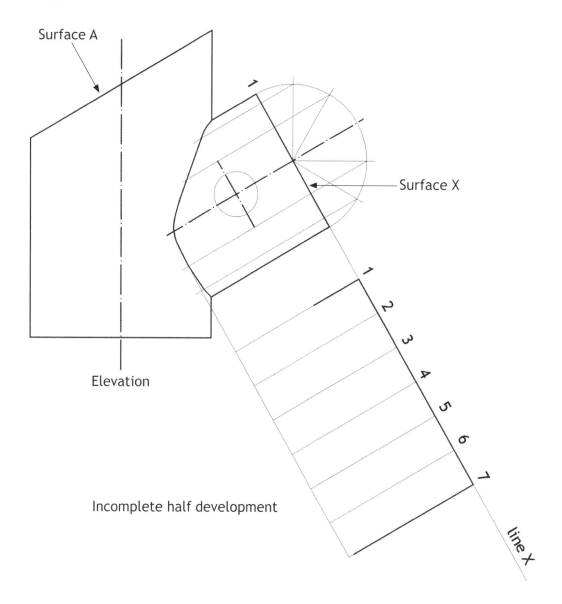

Surface A

Surface X

Elevation

Incomplete half development

line X

Line X has been drawn and will be offset to the left to create a series of parallel lines to locate the intersection for plotting the points.

MARKS | DO NOT WRITE IN THIS MARGIN

5. (continued)

(a) Complete the table provided indicating the offset required to locate the position of the points on each generator given (1–7) and the centre point for the circle.

2

Generator line	Offset from line X (mm)
1	
2	
3	
4	
5	
6	
7	
Circle centre point	

The true shape of surface A is shown below.

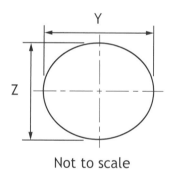

Not to scale

(b) What are the full dimensions for Y and Z on surface A?

1

Y = _____   Z = _____

MARKS | DO NOT WRITE IN THIS MARGIN

6. Use the three layouts in the **Question 6 supplement** provided to answer this question.

Three promotional layouts for "One Stop Kit Shop", a cycling accessories chain, are shown.

The layouts are aimed at three different target markets and will be displayed in three different magazines.

Target market layout 1: (45—65 years) male and female, leisure cycling, working and retired singles and couples, grown-up families, TV influences: gardening and travel shows

Target market layout 2: (25—45 years) male and female, working, keen cyclists, adventure cycling, young families or no family commitments, TV influences: sport and Top Gear

Target market layout 3: (15—25 years) predominantly male, serious adventure and mountain biking, single, independent, TV influences: reality shows, indie and grunge music

The graphic designer has used a range of design elements and principles in each of the three layouts to appeal to the different target markets.

(a) Explain why the styles of typeface used in layout 1 will appeal to its target market.

2

(b) Explain how the use of shape enhances layout 2.

2

MARKS | DO NOT WRITE IN THIS MARGIN

6. (continued)

In layout 2, three lines, two blue and one orange, are used.

(c) Explain how each of these lines improves layout 2. Each of your explanations should be different.   3

Advancing and receding colours have been used in each of the layouts.

(d) Select one of the layouts. Identify an advancing colour used in it, and describe the impact this colour has on the layout.   2

In layout _____ the advancing colour is _____.

The effect this colour has on the layout is:

Different forms of balance have been used in the layouts. In layout 1 the cyclists are placed off-centre, whilst in layout 2 the cyclist is placed in the centre of the layout.

(e) (i) Explain one challenge that placing a main item in the centre of a layout gives the graphic designer.   1

6. (e) (continued)

(ii) Explain the benefit of placing a main item off-centre in a layout (other than your answer to 6(e)(i)).

1

(f) Explain three different ways in which the graphic designer has used design elements and principles in layout 3 to appeal to its target market.

3

MARKS | DO NOT WRITE IN THIS MARGIN

7. Use "The Colour and the Shape" articles (layout A and layout B) from the **Question 7 supplement** provided to answer this question.

A graphic designer has created a magazine double-page spread for a home furnishing publication as shown in layout A. After development, the graphic designer enhanced the layout and produced a pre-press copy, layout B.

(a) Explain **two** reasons for using **headers** and **footers** in a multi-page document.

2

(b) Examine the feature shown below.

(i) State the name of this feature which is in each corner of layout B.

1

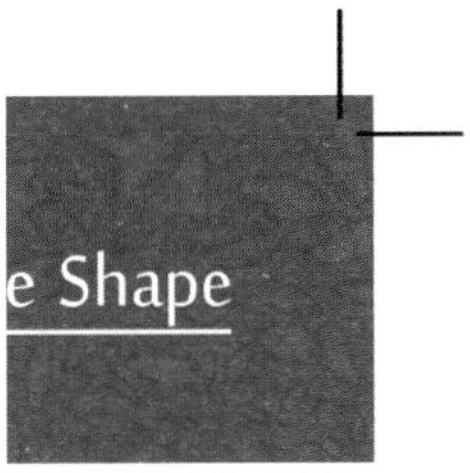

e Shape

(ii) Explain the purpose of this feature.

1

(iii) Explain why the graphic designer used bleed in layout B.

1

7.   (continued)

Examine the layering tree shown below.

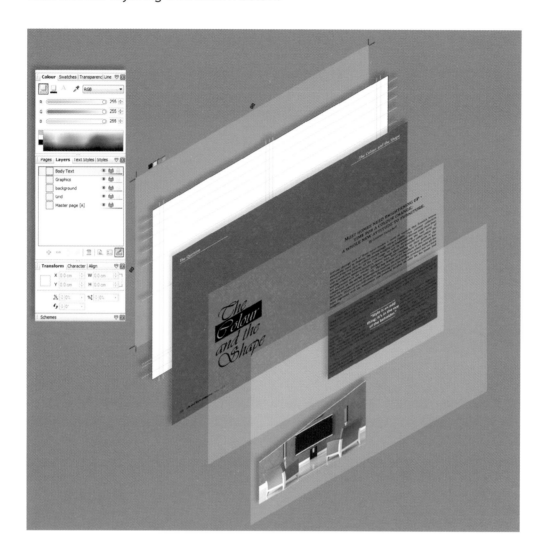

(c)   Describe layering as it is used in layout B in terms of the function and the benefits of layering for the graphic designer.   2

MARKS | DO NOT WRITE IN THIS MARGIN

7. **(continued)**

Examine **both** layout A and layout B.

Three DTP improvements have been made from layout A to layout B.

(d) Identify what these improvements are and explain their impact.

(i) Layout improvement 1 is:

and the impact is:

2

(ii) Layout improvement 2 is:

and the impact is:

2

(iii) Layout improvement 3 is:

and the impact is:

2

[END OF SPECIMEN QUESTION PAPER]

Question 6 supplement

Layout 1

Layout 2

Layout 3

Question 7 supplement

Layout A

Layout B pre-press copy

ADDITIONAL SPACE FOR ANSWERS

MARKS | DO NOT WRITE IN THIS MARGIN

ADDITIONAL SPACE FOR ANSWERS

[BLANK PAGE]

DO NOT WRITE ON THIS PAGE

HIGHER

2015

FOR OFFICIAL USE

H

National
Qualifications
2015

Mark

X735/76/01

Graphic Communication

THURSDAY, 30 APRIL
1:00 PM – 3:00 PM

Fill in these boxes and read what is printed below.

Full name of centre

Town

Forename(s)

Surname

Number of seat

Date of birth
Day   Month   Year   Scottish candidate number

Total marks — 70

Attempt ALL questions.

All dimensions are in mm.

All technical sketches and drawings use third angle projection.

You may use rulers, compasses or trammels for measuring.

In all questions you may use sketches and annotations to support your answer if you wish.

Write your answers clearly in the spaces provided in this booklet. Additional space for answers is provided at the end of this booklet. If you use this space you must clearly identify the question number you are attempting.

Use **blue** or **black** ink.

Before leaving the examination room you must give this booklet to the Invigilator; if you do not, you may lose all the marks for this paper.

SQA

[BLANK PAGE]

DO NOT WRITE ON THIS PAGE

MARKS | DO NOT WRITE IN THIS MARGIN

Total marks — 70

Attempt ALL questions

1.   A CAD Technician created a 3D model of the fire extinguisher, shown below.

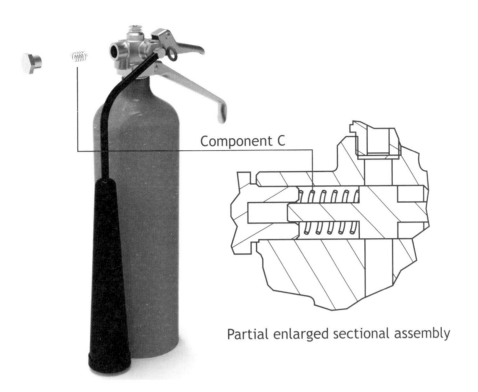

Component C

Partial enlarged sectional assembly

(a) Component C was modelled using 3D CAD.

Describe the 3D CAD modelling technique used to create component C.   2

You may use sketches to illustrate your answer.

1. (continued)

A drawing of the pipe and nozzle sub-assembly is shown below. This was used by the CAD Technician to create models of the individual components.

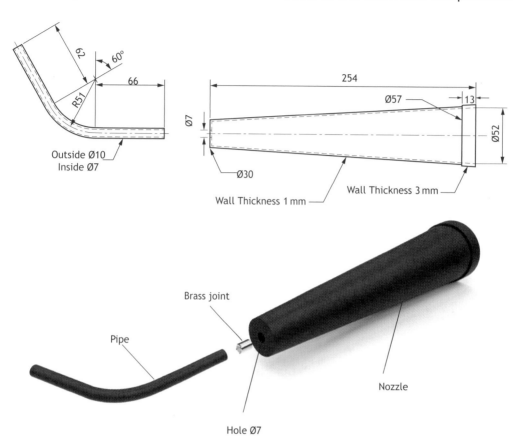

(b) Describe the 3D CAD modelling techniques used to create the **pipe** component. Refer to the dimensions given in the drawing.

3

MARKS | DO NOT WRITE IN THIS MARGIN

1. (continued)

(c) Describe the 3D CAD modelling techniques used to create the **nozzle** component. Refer to the dimensions given in the drawing.

6

[Turn over

1. (continued)

The manufacturer of the fire extinguisher would like to provide a simple wall bracket to hold their product.

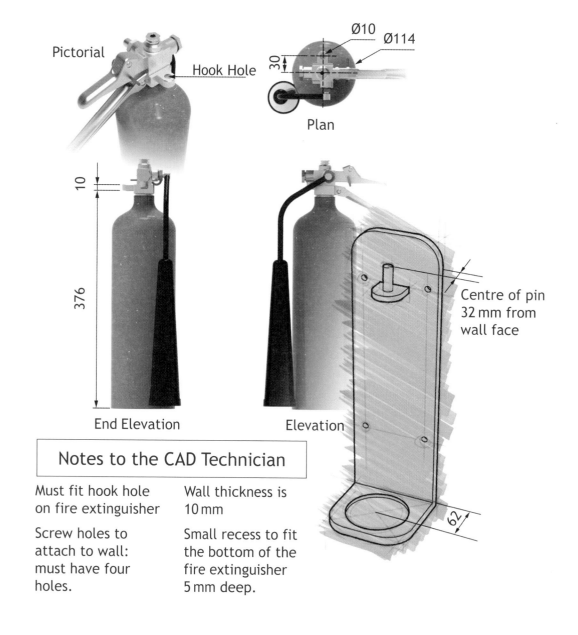

Pictorial

Hook Hole

Ø10 Ø114

30

Plan

10

376

End Elevation

Elevation

Centre of pin 32 mm from wall face

62

Notes to the CAD Technician

Must fit hook hole on fire extinguisher

Screw holes to attach to wall: must have four holes.

Wall thickness is 10 mm

Small recess to fit the bottom of the fire extinguisher 5 mm deep.

MARKS | DO NOT WRITE IN THIS MARGIN

1. **(continued)**

(d) Describe the 3D CAD modelling techniques used to create the wall bracket.

Use measurements from the rendered orthographic and the "Notes to the CAD Technician". You may use sketches to explain your answer.

7

[Turn over

2. Glasgow Riverside Museum opened in 2011. As with any other building built in this country the architecture firm was required to submit a number of different drawings to the local authority to gain planning permission. During this process the architects also produced a number of other graphics for different purposes.

Figure 1

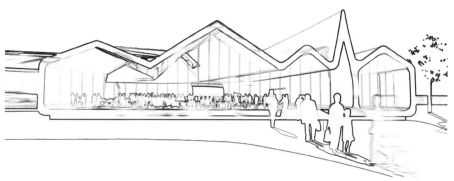

Figure 2

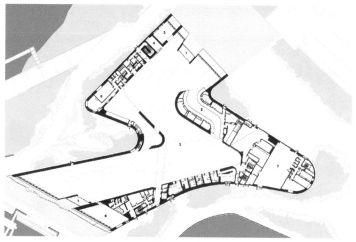

Figure 3

MARKS | DO NOT WRITE IN THIS MARGIN

2. **(continued)**

(a) **Explain**, with reference to the 3P's, the purpose of each of the graphics shown in Figures 1, 2 and 3.

3

The scales commonly used for figure 3 are 1:50 or 1:100.

(b) State **two** factors that influence the choice of scale in this type of graphic.

2

[Turn over

MARKS | DO NOT WRITE IN THIS MARGIN

2. **(continued)**

Sectional views are commonly used in the construction industry.
Cross-hatching is a feature found in sectional construction views.

(c) Describe the benefits of applying cross-hatching to a sectional construction drawing.

2

The standardised construction drawing symbols and conventions shown below are commonly found in many construction drawings.

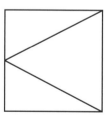
Figure 4

Figure 5

Figure 6

(d) **Identify** each of the symbols/conventions.

3

Figure 4 _____

Figure 5 _____

Figure 6 _____

MARKS | DO NOT WRITE IN THIS MARGIN

3. With the rise in popularity of tablets and smartphones, publishers now produce most of their publications in both hardcopy and digital versions.

(a) **Describe** the advantages to the consumer that the digital format offers over the hardcopy.

2

(b) **Describe** why companies advertising within the publication may prefer the digital format to the hardcopy format.

2

[Turn over

MARKS

3. (continued)

Some publishers are considering moving completely to a digital based distribution of their publications.

(c) **Explain** the disadvantages in the distribution of the digital version over the hardcopy version.

4

[Turn over for Question 4 on *page fourteen*

DO NOT WRITE ON THIS PAGE

4. A furniture designer has produced a 3D CAD illustration of a new table design. The furniture designer needs to prepare the design for manufacture.

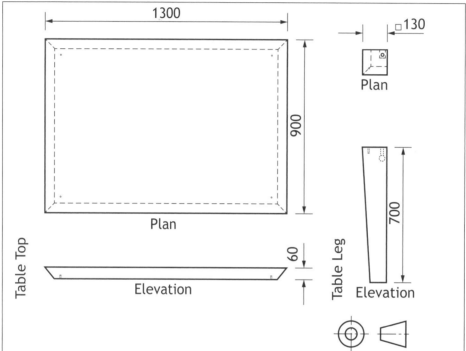

Figure 1

The component drawing of the table top and legs, in Figure 1, are drawn to a scale.

(a) Measure and calculate the scale used for Figure 1. 1

MARKS | DO NOT WRITE IN THIS MARGIN

4.   **(continued)**

The manufacturer has recommended that tolerances be applied to components of the table. They have suggested the following tolerances;

Length of table leg +1·5mm and −0·5mm

Thickness of table top +2·5 mm and −1·5mm

(b) Calculate the maximum and minimum allowable heights of the fully assembled table after applying the tolerances.

2

Maximum height _____ mm   Minimum height _____ mm

(c) Apply the dimensional tolerances to the views below using the correct British Standard conventions.

2

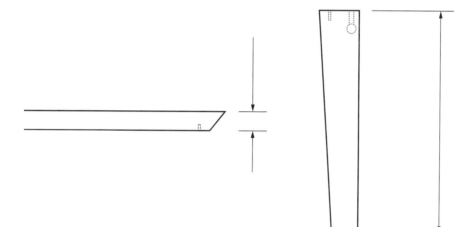

[Turn over

MARKS DO NOT WRITE IN THIS MARGIN

4. (continued)

Knock-down fittings are commonly used in flat-pack furniture design as they make furniture easy to assemble; they require no specialist skills and are easily mass produced. Shown below are the component drawings for two of the most common knock-down fittings used by the retailer (figures 2 and 3) and extracts from the draft assembly instructions (figures 4 and 5).

Wooden Dowel

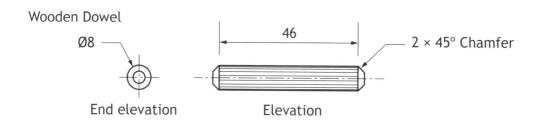

Ø8   46   2 × 45° Chamfer

End elevation   Elevation

Figure 2
(not to scale)

Cam Dowel

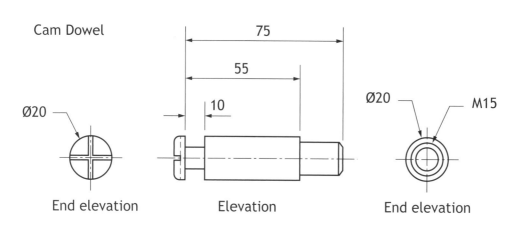

75

55

10

Ø20   Ø20   M15

End elevation   Elevation   End elevation

Figure 3
(not to scale)

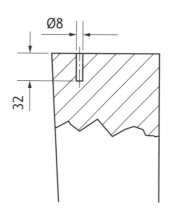

Ø8

32

Figure 4

Exploded view of
assembly method

Figure 5

Enlarged technical drawing of
dowel joint (not to scale)

MARKS | DO NOT WRITE IN THIS MARGIN

4. **(continued)**

The component drawing for the Cam Dowel is incomplete.

(d) Apply the British Standard conventions for the screw threads in each view in Figure 6 below.

2

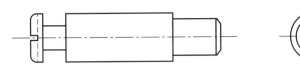

Figure 6

In preparation for manufacture of the table top, the furniture designer has been asked to specify some measurements.

(e) Calculate how far the wooden dowel protrudes from the table leg when fully inserted.

1

_____ mm

(f) Calculate the minimum depth of hole required to be drilled in the table top to accommodate the Cam Dowel.

1

_____ mm

(g) State the type of linear dimensioning used in the elevation view of the Cam Dowel in Figure 3.

1

_____

(h) State the type of the sectional view in Figure 5.

1

_____

[Turn over

MARKS | DO NOT WRITE IN THIS MARGIN

5. Study the magazine pages, read the judges' comments carefully and answer the following questions.

The double page layouts in the magazines have each won graphic design awards.

Below each layout is a comment made by the judges about the success of the layout.

(a)

Judges' comments

"Be yourself – you can't be anyone else", an interview with Kelly Osbourne, takes a dynamic image and combines it with the interview in a simple but effective way. The connection with the young female target market is strong and the use of typeface is creative".

Describe how the designer has used the **headline** to **connect with a target audience** and to **create visual contrast**.

4

5.   (continued)

MARKS | DO NOT WRITE IN THIS MARGIN

(b)

Judges' comments

"The windsurfing layout captures the excitement of the sport while showing a strongly unified layout across both pages. It uses techniques that connect with its young, sporty target audience."

(i)   Explain the ways in which the designer has used DTP techniques to create **unity** in the layout.

2

(ii)   Describe how the designer used DTP features to introduce **proportion** in the layout.

2

5. (continued)

(c)

Judges' comments

"The article about T.I. the American rapper and producer, demonstrates clever use of space. The graphic designer took a photograph which oozes attitude and created a clean and modern layout around it. Also, the designer used several clever and subtle tricks to create contrast and visual impact".

The graphic designer uses **DTP features** to incorporate **shape** in the layout.

Explain how the designer's use of shape improves the layout.   3

MARKS | DO NOT WRITE IN THIS MARGIN

6. A review of music festivals was commissioned by "NEWmusic" magazine. The magazine's readers are in the 18–28 years age range. The musical styles covered by the magazine are "indie" and "rock".

Use the two layouts in the **supplementary sheet for use with Question 6** provided to answer this question.

A graphic designer submitted version 1 of his festival review for consideration but this was not accepted for publication. Version 2 was then developed and was published in "NEWmusic" magazine.

The following questions require you to compare how the designer has applied **design elements** and **principles** in each of the versions and describe the impact they have on the layouts.

Colour is a feature in both layouts

(a) Compare the use of **colour** in the layouts. 2

Alignment is a consideration whenever a layout is created.

(b) Compare the use of **alignment** in both layouts. 4

[Turn over

MARKS | DO NOT WRITE IN THIS MARGIN

6. **(continued)**

Designers choose a style of **balance** to suit the purpose of the layout.

(c) Compare the use of **balance** in both layouts. **2**

Texture can be an important visual feature in a layout.

(d) Compare the use of **texture** in both layouts. **2**

Graphic designers use **emphasis** for a number of purposes.

(e) Compare the use of **emphasis** in both layouts. **2**

[END OF QUESTION PAPER]

ADDITIONAL SPACE FOR ANSWERS

MARKS | DO NOT WRITE IN THIS MARGIN

ADDITIONAL SPACE FOR ANSWERS

National Qualifications 2015

X735/76/11

Graphic Communication
Supplementary Sheet

THURSDAY, 30 APRIL

1:00 PM – 3:00 PM

Supplementary sheet for use with Question 6

Supplementary sheet for use with Question 6

2013

UTunes

Blastin Merry

The UTunes Festival. 30 days of live music from the biggest bands and artists. This jam-packed festival ranged from bands such as Kings of Leon to artists such as Avicii. For anybody who enjoys seeing all of the big bands this is the festival to go to.

Blastin' Merry 2013 sure was a festival to relish. Artists such as Example, Chase and Status, the Rolling Stones, Mumford and Sons and many more contributed to the extremely action packed, enjoyable Festival that everyone seems to know and love. The Rolling Stones made the most impact on festival goers and people of all ages enjoyed their music.

R&R on the Farm

From Headliners such as Rihanna, Mumford and Sons to Jake Bugg and Alt-J, R&R on the Farm made it big this year. A year in which 'R&R' celebrated its 20th anniversary as the biggest and perhaps best Scottish music festival.

Fans were treated to nice weather too which made a welcome and well deserved change to the weather conditions at recent festivals. It all added up to make Galado a magical place for the entire weekend.

Christian Bertrand/Shutterstock.com

Version 1

Page two

Festivals 2013

R&R on the Farm

From Headliners such as Rihanna, Mumford and Sons to Jake Bugg and Alt-J, R&R on the Farm made it big this year. A year in which 'R&R' celebrated its 20th anniversary as the biggest and perhaps best Scottish music festival. Fans were treated to nice weather too which made a welcome and well deserved change to the weather conditions at recent festivals. It all added up to make Galado a magical place for the entire weekend.

Christian Bertrand/Shutterstock.com

Blastin' Merry

Blastin' Merry 2013 sure was a festival to relish. Artists such as Example, Chase and Status, the Rolling Stones, Mumford and Sons and many more contributed to the extremely action packed, enjoyable Festival that everyone seems to know and love. The Rolling Stones made the most impact on festival goers and people of all ages enjoyed their music.

Dziurek/Shutterstock.com

UTunes

The UTunes Festival. 30 days of live music from the biggest bands and artists. This jam-packed festival ranged from bands such as Kings of Leon to artists such as Avicii. For anybody who enjoys seeing almost all of the big bands this is the festival to go to.

Version 2

Page three

[BLANK PAGE]

DO NOT WRITE ON THIS PAGE

HIGHER

2016

FOR OFFICIAL USE

H

National
Qualifications
2016

Mark

X735/76/01

Graphic Communication

TUESDAY, 10 MAY

1:00 PM — 3:00 PM

Fill in these boxes and read what is printed below.

Full name of centre

Town

Forename(s)

Surname

Number of seat

Date of birth

Day   Month   Year   Scottish candidate number

Total marks — 70

Attempt ALL questions.

All dimensions are in mm.

All technical sketches and drawings use third angle projection.

You may use rulers, compasses or trammels for measuring.

In all questions you may use sketches and annotations to support your answer if you wish.

Write your answers clearly in the spaces provided in this booklet. Additional space for answers is provided at the end of this booklet. If you use this space you must clearly identify the question number you are attempting.

Use **blue** or **black** ink.

Before leaving the examination room you must give this booklet to the Invigilator; if you do not, you may lose all the marks for this paper.

XSQA

Attempt ALL questions

Total marks — 70

1. A CAD technician created the 3D CAD model of an electric guitar.

The technician made use of a **CAD Library** in the production of the guitar 3D CAD model.

(a) Describe **two** benefits of using a CAD library.   2

_____

_____

_____

_____

_____

The 3D CAD model of the guitar will be used to create production and promotional graphics.

(b) Describe **one** benefit of using 3D CAD models in:

   (i) Advertising   1

_____

_____

   (ii) Manufacturing   1

_____

_____

1. **(continued)**

MARKS DO NOT WRITE IN THIS MARGIN

An exploded view and a partial enlargement of the guitar are shown below.

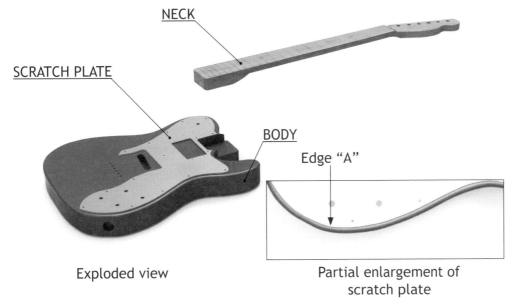

NECK

SCRATCH PLATE

BODY

Edge "A"

Exploded view

Partial enlargement of scratch plate

The CAD technician used the process of **top down modelling** to ensure the neck would fit with the body.

(c) Describe the process of **top down modelling**.

You may use sketches to support your answer.

2

The CAD technician wanted the scratch plate to follow the same shape as the body.

(d) (i) State the name of the 2D CAD tool used to ensure the scratch plate was the same shape as the guitar body at **Edge A**, shown above.

1

_____

(ii) Describe how this 2D CAD tool was used.

You may use sketches to support your answer.

1

[Turn over

1. **(continued)**

A production drawing for a control dial for the guitar is shown below.

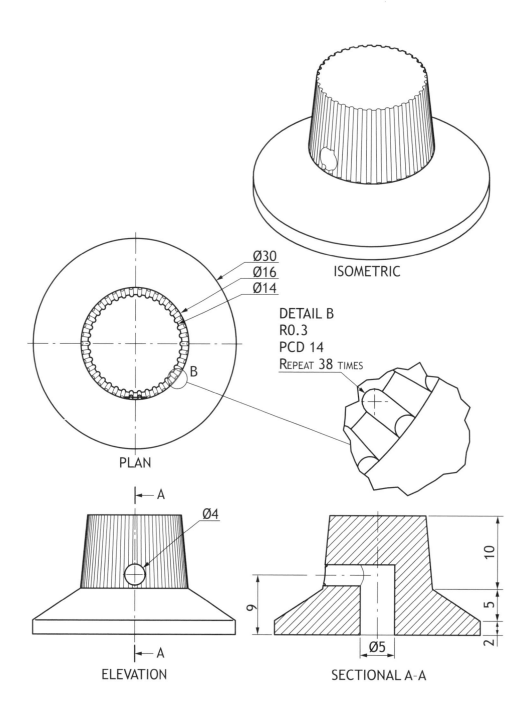

ISOMETRIC

Ø30
Ø16
Ø14

DETAIL B
R0.3
PCD 14
Repeat 38 times

PLAN

A

Ø4

ELEVATION

9

SECTIONAL A-A

10

5

2

Ø5

1. **(continued)**

(e) Describe the 3D CAD modelling techniques required to produce the control dial. Make reference to the dimensions given in the production drawing. You may use sketches to support your answer.

8

1. (continued)

An incomplete elevation and a rendered pictorial drawing of a component of the guitar are shown below.

FLAT

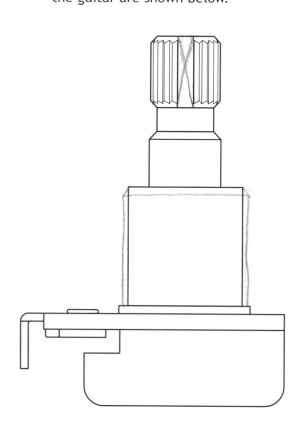

(f) Add the British Standard conventions in the correct location on the incomplete elevation for:

   (i) Thread   1

   (ii) Flat on shaft   1

1. **(continued)**

The headstock for the guitar is shown below. The headstock was modelled using the principles of tangency.

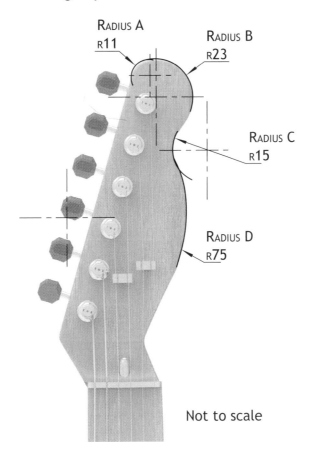

RADIUS A
R11

RADIUS B
R23

RADIUS C
R15

RADIUS D
R75

Not to scale

(g) (i) Calculate the distance from the centre of **radius C** to the centre of **radius D**.

1

(ii) Calculate the distance from the centre of **radius A** to the centre of **radius B**.

1

1. **(continued)**

The 3D CAD model of the guitar neck and a part model are shown below.

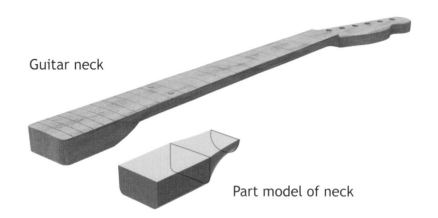

Guitar neck

Part model of neck

(h) Describe the 3D CAD modelling technique used to create the part model of the neck shown above.

3

You may use sketches to support your answer.

2. A fashion magazine, aimed at 25–35 year old females, is producing an article on sunglasses. A graphic designer created a draft layout for the article shown below.

(a) Describe the effects the graphic designer has created in the layout by using the following.

    (i) White Space   2

    (ii) Colour   2

MARKS | DO NOT WRITE IN THIS MARGIN

2. (a) (continued)

(iii) Typeface   2

_____

_____

_____

_____

(b) Explain how the graphic designer has used **proportion** in the layout.   4

_____

_____

_____

_____

_____

_____

_____

_____

(c) Describe how the designer has created **depth** in the layout.   2

_____

_____

_____

_____

(d) Describe how **line** has been used to enhance the layout.   2

_____

_____

_____

_____

2.   (continued)

The Ray Ban logo was made available in a vector file format.

(e) Explain **two** advantages of using a vector file format in the production of the layout.

2

_____

_____

_____

_____

_____

[Turn over

2.   (continued)

The final layout for the article is shown below.

The final layout was produced in layers using DTP software.

MARKS

DO NOT WRITE IN THIS MARGIN

2. **(continued)**

(f) Describe **three** advantages to the graphic designer of using layers for this layout.

3

The graphic designer has used different types of justification for the sub-heading and main body text of the layout.

(g) Explain why the graphic designer has chosen to do this for:

(i) The sub-heading

1

(ii) The main body text

1

[Turn over

2.   (continued)

Pre-Press Layout

The pre-press layout shown above contains crop and registration marks.

(h)   (i)   Explain why the yellow boxes bleed beyond the crop marks.

1

(ii)   Describe the purpose of registration marks in printing.

2

[Turn over for next question

DO NOT WRITE ON THIS PAGE

MARKS | DO NOT WRITE IN THIS MARGIN

3. Dundee Waterfront is undergoing a £1 billion redevelopment.

   The official website includes various types of graphics aimed at promoting the development to the local community. These include:

   - **Location plans** of the entire development
   - **Site plans** of some of the new proposed buildings

   (a) Describe the features for **both** types of plans for providing information about the redevelopment to the local community.

   4

   A selection of rendered CAD pictorial images of the new train station were uploaded to the website.

3. (continued)

MARKS | DO NOT WRITE IN THIS MARGIN

(b) Explain **three** advantages of using rendered CAD pictorials to communicate the design to the local community.

3

The architect shared initial sketches of a building idea on the website. These sketches were created using pencil and marker pen.

(c) (i) Describe how the manual sketches can be converted to digital images for use on the website.

1

(ii) Explain why a **jpeg** would be a suitable file format for these images.

1

More initial sketches were "digitally sketched" on a touch-screen tablet.

(d) Describe **two** advantages to the architect of using digital sketching.

2

[Turn over

MARKS | DO NOT WRITE IN THIS MARGIN

4. An exploded CAD illustration of a castor wheel assembly is shown below.

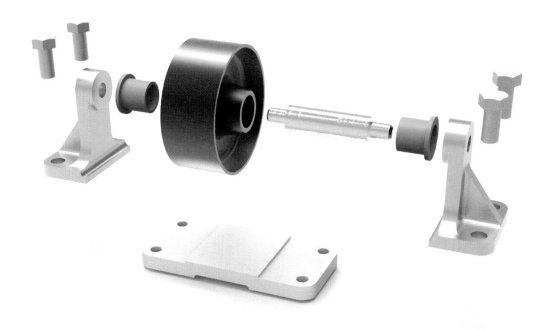

The assembly is made up of several parts that includes four M12 bolts.

The **plan** and **incomplete stepped sectional elevation A-A** are shown on the opposite page.

Complete section A-A by applying hatching lines to appropriate areas in accordance to British Standards.

5

4. (continued)

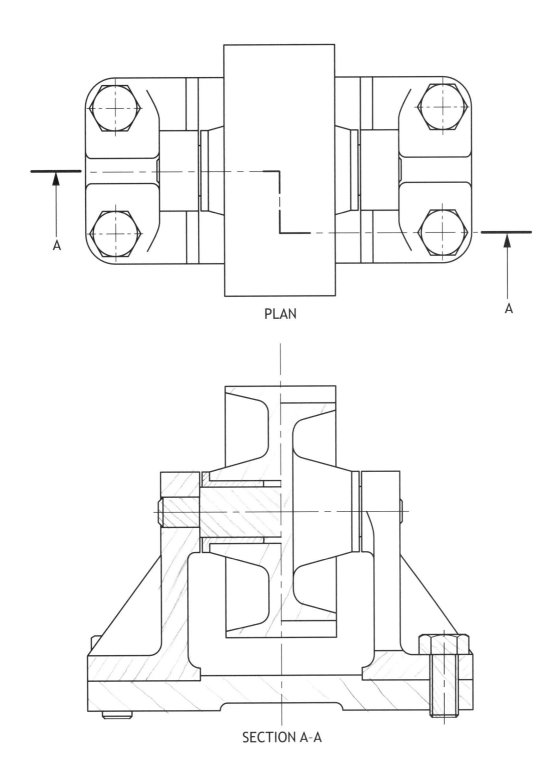

PLAN

SECTION A-A

MARKS | DO NOT WRITE IN THIS MARGIN

5. A building company is planning a new residential area. The plan shown below has been illustrated for potential customers.

Houses 19 to 25 are elevated above others on higher ground.

The drawing does not use **British Standard** conventions.

(a) Identify **three** features of **this drawing** which should be shown on a **British Standards** location plan.

3

_____

_____

_____

5. (continued)

A 3D model of one of the house styles is shown below.

(b) State the total number of houses of this style in the location plan.

1

The architect used the following symbols in drawings of the floor plan

(c) State the correct name for the following symbols.

3

(i) _____   (ii) _____   (iii) _____

[END OF QUESTION PAPER]

MARKS | DO NOT WRITE IN THIS MARGIN

ADDITIONAL SPACE FOR ANSWERS

MARKS DO NOT WRITE IN THIS MARGIN

ADDITIONAL SPACE FOR ANSWERS

[BLANK PAGE]

DO NOT WRITE ON THIS PAGE

Answers

General Marking Principles for Higher Graphic Communication

Questions that ask candidates to "describe"

Candidates must provide a statement or structure of characteristics and/or features. This should be more than an outline or a list. Candidates may refer to, for instance, a concept, experiment, situation, or facts in the context of and appropriate to the question. Candidates will normally be required to make the same number of factual/appropriate points as are awarded in the question.

Questions that ask candidates to "explain"

Candidates must generally relate cause and effect and/or make relationships between things clear. These will be related to the context of the question or a specific area within a question.

Questions that ask candidates to "compare"

Candidates must generally demonstrate knowledge and understanding of the similarities and/or differences between, for instance, things, methods, or choices. These will be related to the context of the question or a specific area within a question.

Candidates can respond to any question using text, sketching, annotations or combinations where they prefer. No marks shall be awarded for the quality of sketching. Marking will relate only to the information being conveyed.

Question			Expected response	Max mark
1.	(a)	(i)	**Re-drawing** Advantages can cover: • option to add in layers • easy to edit/modify • can use in simulations • produces vector graphic • small file size • updated drawings to include modern drawing standards or any other appropriate response. Disadvantages can cover: • very time consuming • mistakes could be made or any other appropriate response. **Scanning** Advantages can cover: • speed • file can be archived • file can be emailed • files are easily viewed on many electronic devices or any other appropriate response. Disadvantages can cover: • drawings cannot be edited after scanning • file sizes • produces raster graphic • physical drawing sizes may prove too large to scan in one attempt (may require piecing together) or any other appropriate advantage/disadvantage.	4
		(ii)	Any relevant explanation made regarding: • the incompatibility of file types • drawing standards • files cannot be worked on simultaneously by different parties • possible complications in language barriers	2
	(b)		Any appropriate and specific aspect for testing such as: • heat flow • flow of people (dynamic) • static loading • strength of material • ventilation flow/rate • light • evacuation time	1

Question			Expected response	Max mark
	(c)		Any appropriate advantage such as: • ease of storage • ease of sharing • ease of collaborative working • positive environmental aspects • reduction in copying or any other appropriate advantage.	1
2.	(a)	(i)	Description which makes reference to: • the loft command to join profiles (1 mark) **and** • the size of the profiles (40 mm x 40 mm) **and** a distance of 120 mm (1 mark)	2
		(ii)	Description which makes reference to: • extruding a cuboid 40 mm and applying a radius to the end edges (1 mark) **and** • drawing a profile on the end of the 3D model, 40 mm x 40 mm (1 mark) **OR** • extruding the profile 40 mm (1 mark) **and** • drawing a profile the shape indicated on the sketch (1 mark)	2

Question		Expected response	Max mark
(b)		A description which makes reference to: • using the shell solid command to remove interior material from the solid model (1 mark) **and** • creating a sketch through the solid model (lengthways). The sketch must be bigger than the solid model (1 mark) **and** • extruding the sketch with a subtraction in one direction and saving the file (1 mark) **and** • redefining the modelling tree/extrusion and subtract in the opposite direction and saving the file under a different name (1 mark) **OR** • creating a sketch through the solid model (lengthways) — the sketch must be bigger than the solid model (1 mark) **and** • extruding the sketch with a subtraction in one direction (1 mark) **and** • using the shell command to remove a face and hollow the model and then saving the file (1 mark) **and** • redefining the modelling tree/extrusion and subtract in the opposite direction and saving the file under a different name (1 mark) or any other suitable **top down** approach in the **correct order.**	4
(c)		An explanation of the appropriateness of inclusion of the item such as: • removes repetition • saves time on drawing common or complex components • common components in a CAD library are likely to conform to standards • accurately represent common or frequently used parts • library components can be used or shared between a wide range of models • library components can be used or shared between a wide range of technicians, operators or people or any other appropriate explanation.	2

Question			Expected response	Max mark
	(d)		An outline description which makes reference to constraining methods, eg:	2
			• centre the axis of two corresponding screw-bosses or centre the axis of the two corresponding radiused case components (1 mark)	
			and	
			• mate the two flat faces on the components, either on the outer case or the bosses (1 mark)	
			OR	
			any other appropriate description.	
	(e)		Production of a modelling plan which communicates how **key** features of the 3D model are generated in relation to the criteria of the question.	4
			Responses should include references to:	
			• 140 mm between centres (1 mark) • minimum 30 mm clearance for handle (1 mark) • 10 mm diameter for the handle (1 mark) • any suitable modelling technique to complete the handle (1 mark)	
			or within any other workable modelling plan.	
3.			Explanations should make appropriate reference to (and relate the choices made to):	4
			• Target market (consumer) 　o families 　o hygiene aware 　o families with young children	
			• Colour scheme/choice of images 　o fresh 　o hygienic 　o calm 　o natural 　o health 　o safety 　o link to broccoli (fresh, organic, natural)	
			• Typeface 　o sans serif font 　o modern 　o use of product logo to promote brand 　o use of uppercase to emphasise the bio/eco aspect of the product	
			or any other appropriate description.	

Question			Expected response	Max mark
4.	(a)	(i)		3
		(ii)	Web	1
		(iii)		1
	(b)	(i)		2
		(ii)	A blind hole is a hole that is drilled or milled to a specified depth without breaking through to the other side of the material.	1
		(iii)	Metric	1
		(iv)	30 mm	1
		(v)	Local or part section	1

Question			Expected response	Max mark
		(vi)		1
5.	(a)			2

Generator line	Offset from line X (mm) (within the ranges)
1	13–15
2	18·5–20·5
3	27·5–29·5
4	37·5–39·5
5	37–39
6	37·5–39·5
7	36·5–38·5
Circle centre point	17–19

Question			Expected response	Max mark
	(b)		Candidate's response must be within the following ranges: X = 57–58 mm Z = 49–51 mm	1
6.	(a)		Explanations such as: • The serif fonts are formal, traditional or old fashioned. • They represent a more sophisticated or mature look to appeal to the older target market. • The flicks and flowing curves in the font styles look friendly and safe to an older target market. • Each letter flowing into the next makes it easier for an older target market to read. Or any other appropriate explanation.	2

Question		Expected response	Max mark
	(b)	Explanations such as: • The page is rectilinear and so are the boxes, lines and the square. • The cropped images create curved or natural shapes that bring eye-catching contrast with/visual interest against the rectilinear shapes. • The cropped cyclist and helmet (the product) stand out against a simple geometric backdrop. • The punctuation circles add contrast against the rectilinear shapes in the layout. **OR** • The curved text above the cyclist creates contrast with the rectilinear shapes in the layout. • The purpose of the advert is to attract attention quickly; the contrasting shapes (mentioned earlier) help ensure this. • The curved text mimics (harmonises with) the shape of the helmet and appears to protect the cyclist's head. Or any other appropriate explanation.	2
	(c)	Explanations such as: The orange line: • creates a unifying accent colour with the other orange items • creates depth by passing behind the cyclist • underlines (emphasises) part of the slogan The blue vertical line: • creates depth by passing behind the helmet • creates eye-catching contrast with the horizontal lines • harmonises with the horizontal blue line • separates the space for the web address The blue horizontal line: • connects the layout items horizontally • aids alignment with the slogan and company name • creates eye-catching contrast with the orange colours • harmonises with the vertical blue line • creates a vertical/horizontal contrast • separates the space for the company name or any other appropriate explanation.	3

Question			Expected response	Max mark
	(d)		The advancing colour is red or orange.	2
			A description such as:	
			The effect this colour has on the layout is that:	
			• it lifts the red or orange items forward	
			• makes the red or orange items more prominent	
			• makes the red or orange items stand out more	
			• creates contrast with the receding colours in the layout	
			or any other appropriate description.	
	(e)	(i)	An explanation such as:	1
			• it leaves two awkward spaces to fill rather than one usable space/it misses the most natural focal points	
			or any other appropriate explanation.	
		(ii)	An explanation such as:	1
			• it will create visual interest through asymmetry, white space, and a natural focal point	
			• it leaves a single space that is easier to fill/populate	
			or any other appropriate explanation.	
6.	(f)		An explanation such as:	3
			• The font is a graffiti/grungy/sans serif style and is fun and youthful.	
			• Images of mountain bike stunts connect with target market.	
			• Tilted images and items make the layout less formal and create visual interest.	
			• Bold, contrasting colours (blue and red) create a youthful look.	
			• Distressed images will appeal to young target market.	
			Or any other appropriate explanation.	
7.	(a)		Explanation for headers and footers such as:	2
			• They can assist in navigating within a document.	
			• They display useful information including, title/chapter, page number, date, author.	
			• They identify the document's content.	
			• They create a sense of unity throughout a document or section.	
	(b)	(i)	Crop marks	1
		(ii)	Explanation such as:	1
			• Crop marks illustrate the boundary where the document is to be cut after printing.	

Question			Expected response	Max mark
		(iii)	Explanation such as:	1
			• To bleed is to extend a graphic or image frame beyond a trimmed edge of the page.	
			• To ensure the graphic or image extends to the very edge of the page of a document.	
			• Edge to edge printing.	
	(c)		Description of layering such as:	2
			• Layering can support in creating a master page for future documents.	
			• Layering allows graphics and text to be edited separately.	
			• Layering supports image manipulation and can occur on separate layers.	
			• Layers can be duplicated and linked to other layers.	
			• Layers can be turned off or on to aid clarity.	
			• Layers can be brought forward or backward as necessary.	
	(d)	(i)	Explanation of impact of use of reverse such as:	2
			• offsets the main text from the headline/sub-headline	
			• lightens the layout (decreases the value)	
		(ii)	Explanation of impact of dropped capital such as:	2
			• emphasises the start of a paragraph	
			• signifies the main text column	
		(iii)	Explanation of impact of when the main text column is converted from one to two columns such as:	2
			• follows a standard method of presenting a main body of text	
			• assists with the readability of the document	

HIGHER GRAPHIC COMMUNICATION 2015

Question		Expected response	Max mark
1.	(a)	**Helix** • Describing a **profile** and **axis** (1 mark). • Describing feature command as **helix** (1 mark).	2
	(b)	**Pipe** • Describing **path**, with all **dimensions** (1 mark). • Describing **profile** with OD10 & ID7 (1 mark). • Feature command as **extrude along a path** (1 mark).	3
	(c)	**Nozzle** **Loft method** • Loft command (1 mark). • Loft from DIA30mm to DIA53 (1 mark). • Offset to 241mm (1 mark). • Loft from DIA57mm to DIA58 offset to 13mm (1 mark). • Shell to 1mm and 3mm (1 mark). • Hole DIA7mm on DIA30mm end (1 mark). **Revolve method** • Ensuring length of part 254mm (1 mark). • Ensuring diameters are DIA30mm DIA53 DIA57 DIA58mm (1 mark). • Ensuring part has a 1mm wall thickness and 3mm end wall thickness (1 mark). • Ensuring profile has correct pipe hole diameter 7mm (1 mark). • Creating a profile axis (1 mark). • Feature command as revolve (1 mark).	6
	(d)	**Wall bracket** • Extruding L-shape bracket (1 mark). • Wall thickness of bracket is 10mm (1 mark). • Circular recess profile is between DIA114mm and 120mm and extrude (subtract) circular recess 5mm deep (1 mark). • Ensuring centre of hook is 32mm from the back of the wall bracket and positioned vertically (1 mark). • Ensuring hook is equal to or less than DIA10mm (1 mark). • Applying four screw holes to bracket (1 mark). • Height from bottom of recess to the bottom of the pin, size 376mm (1 mark).	7

Question		Expected response	Max mark
2.	(a)	**3P's** Figure 1 – **Promotional graphic** • realistic rendering of the building • shows how the completed building will fit in with its environment • promotion or advertising for the building Figure 2 – **Preliminary graphic** • gives a sense of scale and/or form • no specific construction information can be gained • used to give a sense of how the concept may look Figure 3 – **Production graphic** • shows how the building will be laid out • gives details of internal partitions and accommodation *One mark awarded per graphic.*	3
	(b)	**Scale** • size of item • size of paper • degree of detail required *One mark for each correct response.*	2
	(c)	**Cross hatching** • describe different materials • describe different components • show parts that have been cut by the cutting plane *One mark for each correct statement.*	2
	(d)	**BS symbols** Figure 4 – Window hinged at side Figure 5 – Existing tree to be removed Figure 6 – Contours *One mark awarded for each correct response.*	3
3.	(a)	**Advantages to the consumer** Responses should include: • a number of magazines/publications can be stored on a device • easy to zoom in or increase size of font • can be shared across a number of devices for the owner • sharing elements/videos/images on social media or email • instant links to websites (if needed) • can copy and paste content • no need to visit shop or wait for it to be delivered • videos can be embedded • can be read in the dark • available in different languages • better for the environment, with justification e.g. delivery costs, raw materials, printing costs • digital copies cost less than their paper versions to purchase • any other relevant answer *One mark for each correct response.*	2

Question		Expected response	Max mark
	(b)	**Advertising** Responses should include: • sharing elements/videos/images on social media or email • interactivity allows advertisers website to be accessed directly and instantly • potential purchasing of products is easier • live pricing on products • advantage of being able to add videos, animations, slideshows using the same amount of advertising space • any other relevant answer *One mark for each correct response.*	2
	(c)	**Distribution** Responses should include: • adaptability for different platforms/devices • target market limited due to affordability of devices • subscription services • possible loss of jobs for print staff. Not offset by digital based employees • digital rights management • internet access not always available • some potential users put off by digital media and prefer the printed version • any other relevant answer *One mark for each correct response.*	4
4.	(a)	**Scale** 1:20	1
	(b)	**Table height** Max – 764mm Min – 758mm	2
	(c)	**Tolerances** 701,5 / 699,5 or +1,5 / 700 –0,5 +2,5 / 60 –1,5 or 62,5 / 58,5	2
	(d)	**BS threads**	2
	(e)	18mm	1
	(f)	20mm	1
	(g)	Parallel dimensioning	1
	(h)	Part/local Section	1

Question			Expected response	Max mark
5.	(a)		**Connecting with the target audience:** • The use of a slender serif style which looks quite feminine. • The pink accent colour links to female target market. • Overlapping text creates a visually exciting effect. **Creating contrast** • several different typefaces • use of reverse text (white text on black background) • different font sizes • use of capital and lower case • use of serif/sans serif • use of italics/standard • staggered alignment • use of two colours • use of exaggerated quote marks • different line spacing creates visual interest *For full marks* *either:* *1 from **target audience** and 3 from **creating contrast*** *2 from **target audience** and 2 from **creating contrast*** *3 from **target audience** and 1 from **creating contrast***	4
	(b)	(i)	**Creating Unity** • Layering and overlapping one image over another. • The drop cap over the image creates a physical unity. • The use of the yellow accent colour in seven separate areas creates unity through colour. • The angle of the headline matching the angle of the drop cap and the highlighted area of the pull quote. • The graphic images are all on the same theme. *One mark for each correct response for 2 marks.*	2
		(ii)	**Proportion** • The use of a large dominant image on the left hand page leads the eye to the article and its theme. • The size of the title also draws the reader to the article. • The drop cap's proportion leads the reader to the start of the body text. • The change in proportion of the three graphics on the right hand page creates interest and breaks from conformity. *One mark for each correct response for 2 marks.*	2

Question			Expected response	Max mark
	(c)		**Shape** • The column grid structure is rectangular in fact it is almost square. This creates a safe, formal look. • The green circle and the thin circles and add visual contrast against the rectangular structure. • The cropped photograph (or figurative outline) brings a strong irregular shape that suggests movement to the layout and contrasts with the very formal or rectilinear column structure. • The thin circles are not concentric and this creates a sense of movement and pattern that contrasts with the formality of the layout structure. • The full stops and circles used in the layout create rhythm through repetition. *Any three correct responses at one mark each.*	3
6.	(a)		**Colour** **Version 1:** • Too many colours that conflict or contrast with each other. • There is no unifying colour. • There is no accent colour tying the layout together. • Colour used to separate the areas. • Choice of bright colours doesn't suit the target market of 18–28. **Version 2:** • Uses harmonising tones of blue that create unity. • The red headings and sub-heads with the blue create visual interest and unity. • The red text is advancing and stands out. *Any one correct response from each version.*	2

Question			Expected response	Max mark

	(b)		**Alignment**
			
			Version 1:
			• The whole document is centre aligned.
			• The headline is centre aligned along with the 2013.
			• The rule is aligned with the column structure.
			• The sub heads are in alignment within their coloured boxes.
			• The sub-heads are in alignment with the graphics.
			• The body text columns are in alignment with the graphics and the sub-heads.
			• It is a very formal layout.
			• The strong alignment creates a clear structure. that is easy to follow.
			• Fully justified text adds to the strong alignment.
			
			Version 2:
			• The headline and 2013 are centre aligned.
			• The drop caps are all in alignment with the top edge of the text columns.
			• The 'R&R on the farm' sub-head is aligned with the text column.
			• The 'Blastin' Merry' sub-head is aligned with the bottom of the graphic.
			• The white border is centre aligned.
			• The informal layout creates interest.
			
			For full marks
			
			either:
			
			  *1 from **Version 1** and 3 from **Version 2***
			  *2 from **Version 1** and 2 from **Version 2***
			  *3 from **Version 1** and 1 from **Version 2***
				4

	(c)		**Balance** **Version 1:** • Uses a symmetrical balance resulting in a very formal look. • Formal, symmetrical, structure not likely to appeal to the TM. **Version 2:** • Uses an asymmetric balance that creates a youthful feel or look. • It is more of a challenge to find your way around because of the angles and rotated sub-heads. • Asymmetric balance provides visual interest that will appeal to the TM. *Any one correct response from each version.*	2

Question			Expected response	Max mark
(d)			**Texture**	2
			Version 1:	
			• There is a lack of texture in the document.	
			• It is texturally bland and may not appeal to the TM as much as V2.	
			Version 2:	
			• The lined paper effect.	
			• The ink splash top right create visual interest and a course, home-made quality. Their inclusion is intended to appeal to a young TM.	
			• The blurred nature of the ink splash.	
			Any one correct response from each version.	
(e)			**Emphasis**	2
			Version 1:	
			• Uses colour fills to emphasise the names of the festivals.	
			• The layout is flat; there is no use of layering to push items forward and create depth other than the colour fills behind the subheads.	
			• The headline is suitably large and gives emphasis.	
			• The headline is colourful and gives emphasis.	
			• The headline is curved and gives emphasis.	
			Version 2:	
			• The colour fills behind the sub-heads push the sub-heads forward.	
			• The colour fills are rotated to create an angular effect that makes them more obvious.	
			• Drop shadows behind the headline, and images create emphasis.	
			• Drop caps emphasise the start of the body text making it easy to locate where to begin reading.	
			• Contrasting heading font with white outline.	
			Any one correct response from each version.	

HIGHER GRAPHIC COMMUNICATION 2016

Question			Expected response	Max mark
1.	(a)		• Reduce time required to model each component.	2
			• Reduce likelihood of CAD technician making errors.	
			• Represents actual standard component parts.	
			• A library would contain all common component parts.	
			• The same parts would be used by all CAD technicians in the company.	
			• Library components can be used by CAD users worldwide.	
			Any two of the above.	
	(b)	(i)	• Gives a realistic representation of what the final product will look like.	1
			• 3D models can be used to create photorealistic renders.	
			• 3D models can be used to show different materials, colours and textures.	
			• 3D models can be animated.	
			• 3D models can be put into different scenes or contexts.	
			• Used for promotional material (print or digital).	
			Any one from the above.	
		(ii)	• 3D models can be used to directly manufacture (CNC/CAM).	1
			• To enable dimensions to by extracted from the CAD model, without production drawings.	
			• 3D models can be used to show how complex items are assembled.	
			• 3D models do not need a manufacturer to interpret complex production drawings.	
			• Production drawings can be created and fully dimensioned from the CAD model.	
			Any one from the above.	
	(c)		• Top down modelling allows sizes to be captured from another part, without measuring.	2
			• Top down modelling allows geometry (form & shape) to be captured without redrawing.	
			• Top down modelling ensures the 3D CAD model is automatically assembled.	
			• Top down modelling allows the change of one component to automatically update another component.	
			• Components can be created in context within an assembly.	

Question			Expected response	Max mark
(d)	(i)		Use 'Offset' command.	1
	(ii)		Select the bottom edge of the guitar and set a distance.	1
(e)			**Revolve method** • Using the revolve command (1 mark). • Describing the profile to be revolved, with dimensions (1 mark). • Creating a circle on a perpendicular plane and extrude subtract (1 mark). • Describing the dimensioning of circle diameter 4 mm on the perpendicular workplane and its position 9 mm up from the base (1 mark). • Creating diameter 5 mm circle on the base, extrude subtract to 11 mm depth (1 mark). **Creating ridges: Extrude along a path method** • Create circle for ridge on top face (1 mark). • Creating a sketch-path to correct length, extrude-along-a-path (subtract) (1 mark). • Radial Array ridge feature 38 times over PCD 14 (1 mark). **Loft method** • Using the loft command (1 mark). • Describing relevant dimensions, 3 offset distances for 4 workplanes (1 mark). • Creating a circle on a perpendicular plane and extrude subtract (1 mark). • Describing the dimensioning of circle diameter 4 mm on the perpendicular workplane and its position 9 mm up from the base (1 mark). • Creating diameter 5 mm circle on the base, extrude subtract to 11 mm depth (1 mark). **Creating ridges: Loft method** • Create circle for ridge on top face (1 mark). • Creating bottom circle and loft between profiles (subtract) (1 mark). • Radial Array ridge feature 38 times over PCD 14 (1 mark).	8

Question			Expected response	Max mark
(f)	(i)		Correct symbol, correct position (1 mark).	1
	(ii)		Correct symbol, correct position (1 mark).	1
(g)	(i)		90 mm	1
	(ii)		12 mm	1
(h)			Describing using loft command (1 mark). Describing workplanes offset (1 mark). Describing profiles (1 mark).	3
2.	(a)	(i)	• Area of white space underneath 'fab' emphasises the heading and attracts the eye to it. • Area of white space bleeds from left page onto the right. • Area of white space creates breathing space/a rest for the eye. • Areas of white space make the page look less cluttered. Triangular white space creates • Balance • Interest • Rhythm *Any two of the above.*	2
		(ii)	• Warm colour yellow is used that has connotations of summer and warmth. • Harmonious colour scheme. • The repeated use of the colour yellow creates unity in the layout. • Contrast in colours on sunglasses blue and yellow. *Any two of the above.*	2
		(iii)	• Sans serif fonts used for FAB title. Its simplicity works well with the image behind it. • The layout has a combination of serif and sans serif and script fonts creating a stylised feel — reflecting the target market. • Contrasting fonts in the layout create visual interest. *Any two of the above.*	2

(f) ii. Flat symbol

(f) i. Thread detail

Question		Expected response	Max mark
(b)		• Emphasis created by enlarged heading being larger than all other elements. • Triangular images very similar in size, helping to create unity/consistency — also means that no image is more dominant than the other. • Areas of body text are similar in size which helps create consistency and balance. • Enlarged cropped images within triangular frames create visual interest.	4
(c)		• Pictorial/perspective view of the sunglasses themselves gives the illusion of depth against the flat background. • Drop shadow on RayBan logo yellow background. • Drop shadow on sunglasses image. • Drop shadow on bottom yellow box. • Image behind FAB transparency gives depth. • Transparencies added to top-left image creates illusion of depth. • Different sizes of figures in images creates depth. *Any two of the above.*	2
(d)		• The yellow colour of the line creates unity with other yellow elements on the page. • The line draws the reader's eye from left to right and around the image. • The stroke/thickness of the line is consistent and narrow meaning it is not overpowering/dominant. • Angle of lines creates interest/shape on the page. • Lines are used to emphasise the triangular image and the triangular white space. • Lines separate/split elements on the page. *Any two of the above.*	2
(e)		• Scalable without pixelation. • The red background could be easily changed to yellow within the DTP software. Had the image been a bitmap it would have to have been edited using specialist software. • The white text can be made transparent within the DTP software. • The red background could be stretched easily within the DTP software without the need for prior editing in another package. *Any two of the above.*	2

Question		Expected response	Max mark
(f)		• Text and images can be edited separately. • Layers can be turned on and off to improve clarity during the production of the layout. • The mask for 'FAB' could be easily created. • The layers can provide a master-page for similar future layouts. • Edit layers without affecting other parts of the layout. • Layers can be reordered, moved to front, moved to back. *Any three of the above.*	3
(g)	(i)	Centred justification for all the text on the left-hand page creates balance and/or symmetry or alignment or contrast.	1
	(ii)	Fully-justified text provides neatness as there are no 'jagged' edges on the sides of columns.	1
(h)	(i)	No white spaces will appear outside of the yellow boxes after cropping.	1
	(ii)	• To allow the multicolour printing to be set up correctly. • Each register mark should overprint exactly for accurate registration.	2
3.	(a)	Answer should summarise points that will include: **CAD location plans show** • Location of building in relation to streets. • Location of building in relation to other buildings. • Size of building to scale. • Contours show the slope in the land. • Geographical features, eg rivers, woodland, greenbelt. • Position of existing railways, bridges. • North Symbol will show the direction the building is facing. **CAD site plans show** • Proposed building in relation to the property boundaries. • Size and position of the building. • Position of drainage. • Landscape elements. • Gas, electrical and water supplies. • Contours show the slope in the land. • Trees shown in position. • North Symbol will show the direction the building is facing. • Size of the building and site to scale. *Give **two answers from location** and **two from site plan** for the 4 marks.*	4

Question			Expected response	Max mark
	(b)		• Photo real image of how the building will look. • Realistic representation of materials. • Adjacent buildings shown. • Building is shown in its proposed environment. • Shows adjacent roads and direction of traffic flow. • Realistic representations of different lighting conditions day time, night time. • Useful for users who cannot read or interpret 2D drawings such as floor plans, site plans and location plans. • Rendered CAD pictorials can be sent out to the community by email. *Any three of the above.*	3
	(c)	(i)	The sketches would have to be captured/scanned using a suitable device (flatbed, hand, photocopier used as a scanner, digital camera, digitiser/graphics tablet).	1
		(ii)	• Jpeg files are compressed. • Jpeg files are a small size. • Jpeg is a common file type. • Jpegs are easily accessible without any specialist software.	1
	(d)		• The sketches could include realistic material representations. • They can be built up in a series of layers to ease editing. • They are automatically stored electronically and do not require scanning to upload to the website. • Able to show client changes instantly. • Sketches can be exported into other packages. • Easy to share through email. *Any two of the above.*	2
4.			1 mark for each correctly sectioned component (5 in total). ▲ 1 mark Pulley ✱ 1 mark Bush ● 1 mark Left bracket ■ 1 mark Base ● 1 mark Right bracket SECTION A-A	5

Question			Expected response	Max mark
5.	(a)		• Symbols for existing trees **OR** proposed trees **OR** trees to be removed **OR** trees accepted • North symbol • Contour lines • Boundary lines *Any three of the above.*	3
	(b)		Four	1
	(c)	(i)	Insulated board, insulation board	1
		(ii)	Towel rail	1
		(iii)	Drainage	1

Acknowledgements

Permission has been sought from all relevant copyright holders and Hodder Gibson is grateful for the use of the following:

Image © Joanna Zopoth-Lipiejko/Shutterstock.com (SQP page 10);
Image © Alex James Bramwell/Shutterstock.com (SQP page 10);
Image © Dudarev Mikhail/Shutterstock.com (SQP page 22);
Image © pio3/Shutterstock.com (SQP page 22);
Image © Monkey Business Images/Shutterstock.com (SQP page 22);
Image © Warren Goldswain/Shutterstock.com (SQP page 22);
Image © l i g h t p o e t/Shutterstock.com (SQP page 22);
Image © Sergey Lavrentev/Shutterstock.com (SQP page 22);
Image © archideaphoto/Shutterstock.com (SQP page 23);
Three images of the Gasgow Riverside Museum of Transport. Reproduced by permission of Zaha Hadid Architects (2015 page 8);
An extract from Cosmopolitan, September 2013. Interview by Elaine Lipworth & photograph by James White © Cosmopolitan Magazine UK (2015 page 18);
An extract from Extreme sports magazine. Design: danmackay.com.au (2015 page 19);
An extract from Vibe Magazine, May 5, 2007. Article by Hillary Crosley & photo by Kaseem Black (2015 page 20);
Image © Maxim Blinkov/Shutterstock.com (2015 Supplementary Sheet);
Image © Dziurek (2015 Supplementary Sheet);
Image © Christian Bertrand/Shutterstock.com (2015 Supplementary Sheet);
Image © melis/Shutterstock.com (2015 Supplementary Sheet);
The logo for Ray-Ban © Luxottica Group S.p.A. (2016 pages 9, 11, 12 & 14);
Image © Rhea Bue (Shades of Style) (2016 pages 9, 12 & 14);
Two images © Nicoll Russell Studios (2016 page 16).